ALIEN SIGHTINGS AND ENCOUNTERS

by Jenny Mason

12
STORY LIBRARY
MORE TO EXPLORE

www.12StoryLibrary.com

12-Story Library is an imprint of Bookstaves.

Developed and produced for 12-Story Library by Focus Strategic Communications Inc.

Library of Congress Cataloging-in-Publication Data
Names: Mason, Jenny (Children's author), author.
Title: Alien sightings and encounters / by Jenny Mason.
Description: Mankato, Minnesota : 12-Story Library, 2022. | Series: Aliens! |
Includes bibliographical references and index. | Audience: Ages 10–13 | Audience: Grades 4–6
Identifiers: LCCN 2020014921 (print) | LCCN 2020014922 (ebook) | ISBN 9781632359315 (library binding) |
ISBN 9781632359667 (paperback) | ISBN 9781645820970 (pdf)
Subjects: LCSH: Unidentified flying objects—Juvenile literature. | Human-alien encounters—Juvenile literature.
Classification: LCC TL789.2 .M35 2022 (print) | LCC TL789.2 (ebook) | DDC 001.942—dc23
LC record available at https://lccn.loc.gov/2020014921
LC ebook record available at https://lccn.loc.gov/2020014922

Photographs ©: Fer Gregory/Shutterstock.com, cover; Lena Graphics/Shutterstock.com, 1; Chronicle/Alamy, 4; Crobard~commonswiki/PD, 4; JMK/CC4.0, 5; PD, 5; Lena Graphics/Shutterstock.com, 6; XX, 6; Bobby Gooner/YouTube.com, 7; ktsdesign/Shutterstock.com, 7; J.S. Henrardi/PD, 8; J2R/Shutterstock.com, 9; NASA, 9; U.S. Army Photo, 10; U.S. Air Force, 11; Library of Congress, 11; Taras Young/CC4.0, 12; Paul's Pursuits/YouTube.com, 13; XX, 14; CNN/YouTube.com, 14; CNN/YouTube.com, 15; Gorodenkoff/Shutterstock.com, 15; Fesus Robert/Shutterstock.com, 16; Bizarre and Grotesque/YouTube.com, 17; Andrew Harker/Shutterstock.com, 17; AuntSpray/Shutterstock.com, 18; Pavel Tvrdy/Shutterstock.com, 18; LSST/CC4.0, 19; Topham Partners LLP/Alamy, 20; COLUMBIA PICTURES/Ronald Grant Archive/Alamy, 21; matrioshka/Shutterstock.com, 22; Olek95/PD, 23; Silentlight87/CC4.0, 23; KOAA 5/YouTube.com, 24; lukeruk/Shutterstock.com, 24; XX, 25; Pictorial Press Ltd/Alamy, 25; petrmalinak/Shutterstock.com, 26; Kristina Blokhin/Alamy, 27; tonynetone/CC2.0, 27; XX, 28; XX, 29; Dotted Yeti/Shutterstock.com, 29

About the Cover
Man rudely awakened by an alien.

Table of Contents

1 Kenneth Arnold: A UFO Craze Begins

Kenneth Arnold flew his plane a lot for his work as a salesman. He used it to reach customers in remote areas around the state of Washington. On June 24, 1947, Arnold was flying over the scenic glaciers atop Mt. Rainier when he saw something strange.

Kenneth Arnold next to his aircraft in 1947.

Nine glowing objects whizzed across the sky. The objects moved at impossible speeds. Arnold thought they were moving at around 1,200 miles per hour (1,930 km/h).

Arnold told a reporter the objects moved like stones or saucers skipping across water. When the story hit front pages across the country, the headlines called the objects

An artist's illustration of how the saucers moved across the sky.

"flying saucers." For weeks and years to come, saucer sightings broke out across the country.

THINK ABOUT IT

Once Arnold's story went public, why do you think the press did not want to change the name from flying saucers to flying boomerangs?

96

Percentage of Americans who had heard of flying saucers by 1966

- Nearly half the nation believed flying saucers were real.
- Kenneth Arnold tried to correct the description. The press ignored his flying boomerangs.
- Artist Frank R. Paul drew fantastic flying saucers on magazine covers. His images date back to 1929.

Magazine cover illustrated by Frank R. Paul.

2

Ariel School, Zimbabwe: An Alien Playground

Little men interrupted recess. They exited their spaceships. About 60 children at the Ariel School in Zimbabwe, Africa saw the aliens on September 16, 1994. The children were between the ages of 6 and 12. The aliens did not speak. They stared at the children with their big black eyes. The children screamed and ran away to alert their teachers.

The adults doubted the children's story. Even so, John E. Mack traveled from the

John E. Mack.

John E. Mack interviewed many of the children at the Ariel School.

US to interview the students. He was a famous psychiatrist and alien researcher. He believed that many of the people he talked to had seen things that could not easily be explained.

15

Minutes of light from a meteor shower that flew over South Africa on September 14, 1994

- Dozens reported spaceships flying behind the blazing meteors.
- Many people saw aliens after the meteor shower. Multiple sightings are called a flap.
- Cynthia Hind was South Africa's official UFO detective. She notified Mack about the Ariel School aliens.

THE CHINESE PEARL

A UFO visited 11th-century China. A large ball landed. Its door opened. Inside and out, the pearl was as bright as the sun. Locals saw the pearl often over a period of 10 years. Then, for no known reason, it disappeared.

3

A Belgian UFO Wave?

The flying triangle photographed during the Belgian UFO wave.

Belgium became the center of a surge of UFO sightings in 1989 and 1990. The first event took place in November 1989. Thousands across the country saw strange lights in the sky. Some saw a triangular object hovering.

Then a photograph fueled news frenzy. It clearly showed a dark, triangular aircraft with four bright rocket thrusters.

The following year, many witnesses saw multiple objects streaking across the skies. Military radar picked up the objects, too. Fighter jets were sent to investigate, but they could not find anything.

A small shop in Brussels displays UFO objects in its window.

Then, in 2011, the military revealed that these objects were pieces of an old satellite. The photograph was also a hoax. As a prank, some teenagers painted and decorated a sheet of plastic to look like an alien spaceship.

13,500

Number of Belgians estimated to have seen the mysterious objects

- On average, one satellite crashes to Earth every week.
- China's space lab, Tiangong-2, crashed on July 19, 2019.
- Russia's *Mir* space station crashed in 2001. As large as six school buses, it is the biggest satellite to crash so far.

Mir space station.

4

Project Blue Book: Investigating UFO Reports

The US Air Force had to do something. Reports of strange objects were flooding in. What were these flying objects? Was the nation in danger?

Project Sign was set up in 1948 to investigate all UFO reports. Most mysteries were solved. Many of the cases turned out to be asteroids, weather balloons, or hoaxes.

In 1951, the team became known as Project Blue Book. They solved many cases. Then, Blue Book ran into trouble. Police in Ohio reported a silver disk

This 1951 weather balloon was originally thought to be a UFO.

1,501
Number of UFO cases reported in 1951

- Project Blue Book investigated a total of 12,618 sightings. 701 were never solved.
- Captain Edward J. Ruppelt was Blue Book's first commander. He invented the phrase UFO.
- Project Blue Book's investigators were the original "Men in Black."

The staff of Project Blue Book, 1963.

shape in the sky in 1966. The Blue Book team didn't believe the report. However, the media thought the report could be real.

Finally, the government stepped in. In 1969, they shut down Project Blue Book.

ALIEN VOTERS

In 1977, Jimmy Carter became the 39th US president. Eight years earlier, he saw a bright colorful object in the night sky in southern Georgia. Carter did not report the incident for several years. Years later, he said that he did not believe it was an alien spacecraft.

5

Rendlesham Forest: Aliens vs. the Military

Photo of red UFOs taken in 2005.

The Rendlesham Forest in England was cold the night of December 26, 1980. Two US Air Force bases operated in those woods. Some airmen out on patrol saw unusual lights. They called for backup. The team hiked deep into the dark forest.

They saw red and blue pulsing lights. Then, a blinding white light flashed on them. Some airmen dropped to the

The gate of the Rendlesham Forest, where the UFO incident occurred.

A sculpture of the UFO witnesses saw, including its unusual markings (right), is located at the site.

ground. One saw a triangular ship. Maybe it was hovering. Maybe it stood on posts. Swiftly, the ship flew away.

The next night, the strange lights returned. Another team searched the forest. They saw the same lightshow until daybreak. Years later, a UFO investigator discovered that the lights came from nearby safety lights and a lighthouse.

7

Length in inches (18 cm) of the dents the spacecraft pressed in the soil

- A local farmer recognized the dents as rabbit diggings.
- Meteors are often mistaken for UFOs. A very bright meteor sailed over England on December 26, 1980.
- The spaceship reportedly scraped trees when it flew away. The marks were actually axe cuts.

THINK ABOUT IT

The Rendlesham witnesses had different memories of the same event. How is that possible?

6

Tipped Off: Military Secrets Exposed

In 2017, two facts shocked the world. First, the US Navy had multiple UFO encounters. Second, a secret government team had been tracking UFOs. They operated from 2007 to 2012.

Luis Elizondo tipped off reporters. He was a former intelligence officer. He was also in charge of the secret team. It was called the Advanced Aerospace Threat Identification Program (AATIP). AATIP investigated intelligent aliens and enemy aircraft. They had to determine which was a greater threat.

Some countries are allies to the US. Others are enemies.

Luis Elizondo.

$22 million

Amount AATIP spent over five years

- Elizondo shared three shocking AATIP videos with reporters in 2017.
- The videos were shot from US Navy fighter jets. They encountered UFOs over the ocean.
- The objects flew at impossible speeds. One bounced above the water, making foamy waves.

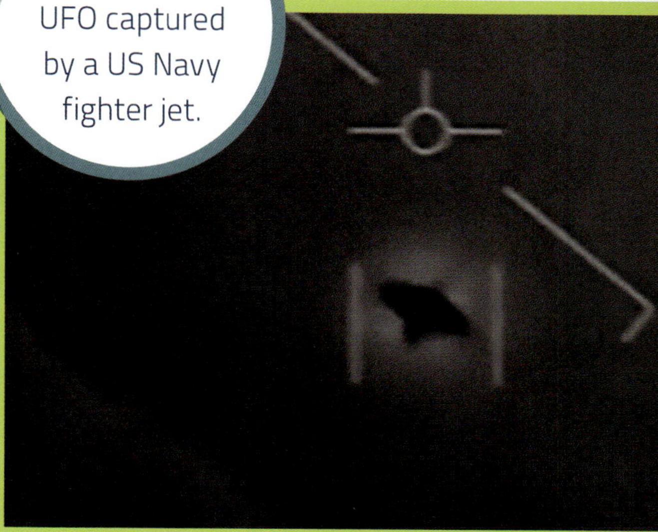

An image of a UFO captured by a US Navy fighter jet.

AATIP had to find out if aliens would be allies or enemies. Most of their discoveries turned out to be human-made spy drones. Some were test missiles. They never found aliens.

In April 2019, the US Navy began a new program. It would give pilots a way to report UFOs.

Military spy drones are sometimes mistaken for UFOs.

7

Valensole: Aliens in France

The Provence region in southern France is colorful. Purple lavender fields stretch for miles. Every July, tourists cannot pass it up. In 1965, neither could aliens.

Maurice Masse worked in the Valensole lavender fields. Early on July 1, 1965, he heard an odd whistling. He traced the sound to an egg-shaped spaceship. It was as big as a car and stood on four posts.

Two small beings with big eyes exited the ship. They wore gray-green suits. They stunned Masse with a device. Unable to move, Masse watched the

Illustration showing Masse's encounter with the aliens.

2,806

Number of UFO sightings in France from 1954 to 2019

- GEIPAN is France's national UFO review team. It shares all data with the public.
- Only 101 incidents have stumped the team.
- Aimé Michel was France's top ufologist. He could not debunk Masse's encounter.

beings browse the lavender flowers. He heard them grumbling. Finally, they flew away. Detectives found the dents where the ship landed. The nearest plants died, too. The local officials believed Masse was telling the truth.

A NEW CROP OF ALIENS

Crop circles seemed like alien messages. They were huge, complex designs stamped into grain fields. In 1991, two men claimed responsibility. Other artists around the world also created crop circles.

8

Oumuamua: An Alien Buoy

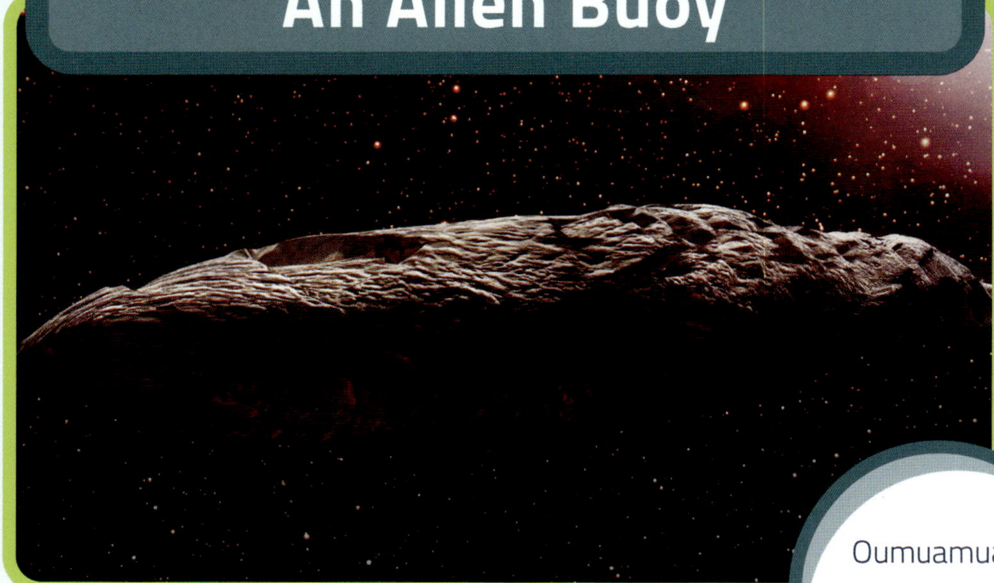

Oumuamua is about 800 feet (230 m) long.

Astronomers only glimpsed the first space object from another star system. A telescope in Hawaii spotted the object on October 19, 2017.

Hawaii's telescope sits at the top of Mauna Kea.

37

Number, in billions, of stars and galaxies the Large Synoptic Survey Telescope (LSST) hopes to see

- With a mirror the size of a tennis court, the LSST will scan space for more objects like Oumuamua.
- Avi Loeb suspected intelligent life crafted Oumuamua.
- Oumuamua reflected lots of light. It could be a space probe pushed by light particles.

Pieces of glass are placed into a mold to make the LSST mirror.

Scientists named the object Oumuamua. This is the Hawaiian word for scout or messenger.

It was a reddish thin slab. It seemed to rocket past Earth. In every way, Oumuamua was bizarre. Still, most astronomers agreed it was a space rock.

Avi Loeb, the world's leading astronomer, disagreed. Oumuamua did not whoosh by us. It floated in space the way a buoy floats in the ocean. Plus, the object flashed like a beacon. Loeb thought it might be an alien space probe. Loeb's theories rocked the scientific community.

SHOOT FOR THE STARS

The Breakthrough Starshot project will launch a nanocraft, or extra small space probe, by 2036. Starshot will snap pictures of the planet Proxima Centauri b. Proxima b is an exoplanet that is 4.2 light years away.

9

J. Allen Hynek: The First UFO Scientist

J. Allen Hynek was the Sherlock Holmes of UFO sightings. He helped the military solve puzzling alien mysteries. He pursued this work from 1948 to 1969.

The US Air Force received many UFO reports in 1947. They began to track and solve UFO cases. They needed an expert scientist to investigate the strange events. They chose Hynek because he was a top astronomer.

Hynek used science to solve cases. He was the first to classify alien encounters. He found three kinds of Close Encounters (CEs). CEs of the

J. Allen Hynek in 1973.

first kind included UFOs seen up close. If UFOs left behind burn marks or landing prints, they were considered CE-2 types. CE-3 types included actual alien contact.

$20 million

Amount spent to make the 1977 movie *Close Encounters of the Third Kind*

- J. Allen Hynek's CE scale inspired the movie. It made nearly $170 million in the US.
- Hynek advised the moviemakers. He also appeared briefly in the movie.
- Hynek began UFO research as a doubter. Over time, he decided to keep an open mind.

A scene from *Close Encounters of the Third Kind.*

10

Distant Horizons: Ancient Aliens

Aliens gave light bulbs to ancient Egyptians. They also shared their flying machines. Historians took these ideas from Egyptian hieroglyphs, or carvings. One temple seemed to show helicopters and spaceships. Another displayed a light bulb.

The carvings were misunderstood. The flying machines result from an illusion. Newer hieroglyphs carved on top of older ones made it look like UFOs. The light bulb was a bubble under water.

Mistranslated Bible passages led researchers to think aliens in a spaceship

An ancient fresco that appears to show Egyptians were visited by an alien spaceship.

Hieroglyphs appear to show modern aircraft on this ancient Egyptian temple.

were mentioned. A man saw bizarre creatures flying a machine. It had spinning wheels like propellers. The creatures were actually angels. The wheels were sparkling stones.

12

Age of K'inich Janaab' Pakal when he became a Mayan king in 615 CE

- Carvings on Pakal's coffin lid seemed to show him flying a spaceship.
- The image is similar to photos of astronaut John Glenn in a 1960s space capsule.
- Again, historians needed a closer look. Pakal was dropping into the underworld.

A BONE TO PICK

Some sightings include dead aliens. Or so researchers thought. They discovered long misshapen skulls around the world. The skulls were human. They had been stretched while the person was young. Some cultures find long skulls beautiful.

11

The 37th Parallel: The UFO Highway

Chuck Zukowski.

Chuck Zukowski picked up an unusual hobby as a teenager. He loved investigating UFO and alien cases. All his life, he was like a real-world Agent Mulder. Mulder is a character on the popular TV show The *X-Files*.

Zukowski realized the Earth had a UFO Highway. It ran 37-degrees north of the equator. This region is called the 37th Parallel.

Here, more than anywhere, weird things seem to happen.

Area 51 sits on the UFO Highway. Cattle herds are drained of blood. Strange lights and UFOs have been spotted from Delaware to California. Many Native American cultures have sacred sites along this line. Called sipapus, they are where the ancestors are believed to have arrived.

The 37th Parallel.

Some rose from the earth. Others came down from the stars.

THINK ABOUT IT

Have you ever seen something strange in the sky? Besides a UFO, what else do you think it could it have been?

35

Percent of Americans who think aliens visit Earth

- About 16 percent have seen a UFO.
- *The X-Files* once held the record for longest-running science fiction TV show. It first aired in September 1993.
- The show is about alien encounters.

The X-Files, the original series, ended in 2002 but was revived in 2016 and 2018.

12

E.T. Goes Home: UFO Sightings Decline

Some government departments recently opened up about UFOs and aliens. They shared many secret documents. Plus, millions of people carry smart phones with cameras. Anyone can record UFO or alien sightings.

Even so, UFO and alien sightings have decreased, a lot. The peak came in 2014. That year, over 8,000 reports came in from around the world. Reports dropped every year after that. In 2019, there were only about 3,000 sightings. Many UFO clubs are closing because they don't have enough members.

What has caused this worldwide decline? Governments sharing secrets with the public is one cause. All those smart phones are

Alien-themed gift shops are still popular in Roswell, NM.

another. Because of the Internet, it is easier than ever to debunk UFO and alien sightings.

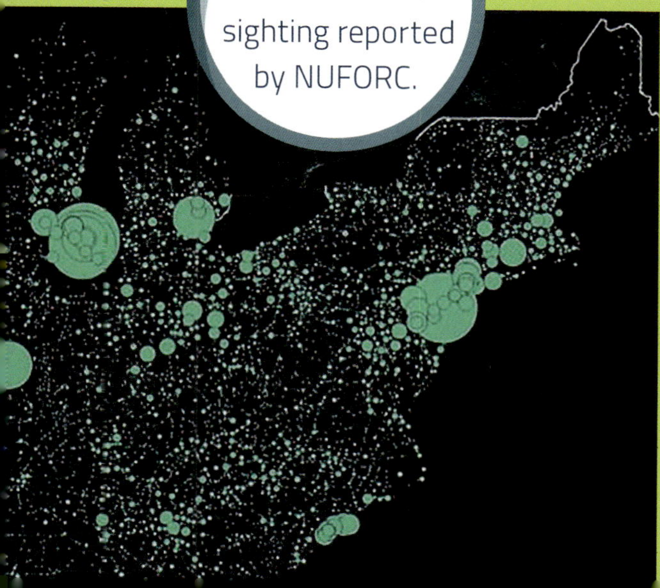

Each green circle is a UFO sighting reported by NUFORC.

1974

Year the National UFO Reporting Center (NUFORC) began tracking alien and UFO encounters

- NUFORC has received a grand total of 130,000 reports from around the world.
- It provides a 24-hour hotline. People can also make a report online.
- NUFORC finds that most UFO sightings happen in the summer when people are outside more.

Above and Beyond

The Delphos Ring.

The Delphos Ring

On November 2, 1971, Ron Johnson saw a bright blob in the sky. There was also a glowing ring on the ground. It measured about eight feet (2 m) across. The ring was not a landing site. It was a type of fungus. The bright blob was a type of lightning.

MUFON
Mutual UFO Network

Mutual UFO Network

MUFON began in 1969. It is the world's oldest and largest UFO detective team. It has 4,000 members across 43 countries and all 50 states. They also have a live, UFO sightings map online.

UAP or UFO

UFO stands for unidentified flying object. The term invites negative stereotypes. That is why the military calls them unidentified aerial phenomena, or UAPs.

Glossary

aerospace
An industry that deals with travel beyond Earth's atmosphere.

asteroid
A small rocky object that orbits a star.

beacon
A strong light or signal that can be detected from far away.

boomerang
A flat, curved wooden object that circles back after being thrown in the air. Originally used for hunting animals.

buoy
An object that floats in one place in a body of water.

capsule
A small container in spaceships where astronauts live or work.

comet
A ball of ice and dust that heats and flares as it approaches the sun.

equator
An imaginary line around Earth's center, forming equal distance between the North and South Poles.

frenzy
A wild or uncontrolled activity.

hoax
An act that is meant to trick or deceive people.

satellite
A human-made object that orbits the Earth. It is used to get information.

psychiatrist
A doctor who treats mental or emotional illness.

Read More

Betts, Bruce. *Super Cool Space Facts: A Fun Fact-filled Space Book for Kids*. Emeryville, CA: Rockridge Press, 2019.

Hile, Lori Elizabeth. *Investigating Unsolved Mysteries. Aliens and UFOs: Myth or Reality*. North Mankato, MN: Capstone Press, 2018.

McCollum, Sean. *Paranormal Handbooks.* The Paranormal Handbook to UFOs, Crop Circles, and Alien Encounters. Chicago, IL: Raintree, 2016.

Pascoe, Elaine. *Fooled You!: Fakes and Hoaxes Through the Years.* New York: Henry Holt, 2016.

Pipe, Jim. *The Twilight Realm*. Aliens. New York: Gareth Stevens, 2013.

Visit 12StoryLibrary.com

Scan the code or use your school's login at **12StoryLibrary.com** for recent updates about this topic and a full digital version of this book. Enjoy free access to:

- **Digital ebook**
- **Breaking news updates**
- **Live content feeds**
- **Videos, interactive maps, and graphics**
- **Additional web resources**

Note to educators: Visit 12StoryLibrary.com/register to sign up for free premium website access. Enjoy live content plus a full digital version of every 12-Story Library book you own for every student at your school.

Index

About the Author

Jenny Mason has always lived in UFO country. She grew up a few hours from Roswell, New Mexico. She currently lives in Colorado near the UFO Highway. She will go anywhere in search of amazing stories.